This publication is dedicated to my mother
Florance Dixon Daniels, father Reginald Lynch
and my darling daughter Bella Lee.

Sasha S. Dixon, Author and artist, from Cleveland Heights, OH. Currently a student majoring in Studio Art at The University Of Akron. Author of *Charm and Passion*, developed a love for education after becoming a mother.

Skyler S. Warren, Artist who also designed the cover of *Charm and Passion* was born in Sandusky, OH, where he developed his love for the arts. Majoring in studio arts, Skyler geared his focus toward graphic design during his time at the University of Akron. Skyler continues to develop his skills working as a graphic designer and illustrator helping other throughout his career.

Email - ssd11@zips.uakron.edu
Facebook - @sashadixon19
Twitter - @SashaDixon19
Instagram - @sashadixon19

ISBN 9780692863930

Library of Congress Control Number: 2017904542

Printed in the United Sates of America March 2017

123

With Bella Lee

THIS IS THE NUMBER **ONE!**

ONE

THIS IS THE WORD **ONE**.

THIS IS **ONE** CIRCLE!

THIS IS THE NUMBER **TWO!**

TWO

THIS IS THE WORD **TWO**!

HERE ARE **TWO** CIRCLES!

THIS IS THE NUMBER **THREE!**

THREE

THIS IS THE WORD **THREE!**

HERE ARE **THREE** CIRCLES!

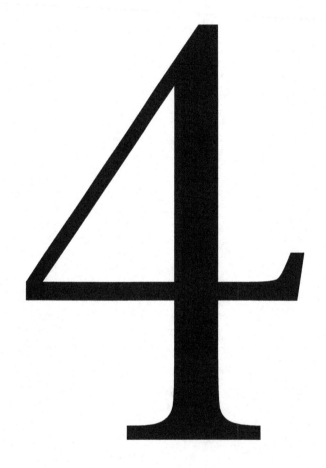

THIS IS THE NUMBER **FOUR!**

FOUR

THIS IS THE WORD FOR THE NUMBER **FOUR!**

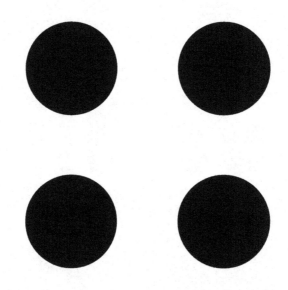

HERE ARE **FOUR** CIRCLES!

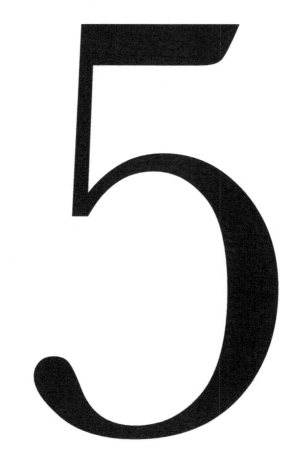

THIS IS THE NUMBER **FIVE!**

FIVE

THIS IS THE WORD **FIVE!**

HERE ARE **FIVE** CIRCLES!

THIS IS THE NUMBER **SIX!**

SIX

THIS IS THE WORD **SIX!**

HERE ARE **SIX** CIRCLES!

THIS IS THE NUMBER **SEVEN!**

SEVEN

THIS IS THE WORD **SEVEN**!

HERE ARE **SEVEN** CIRCLES!

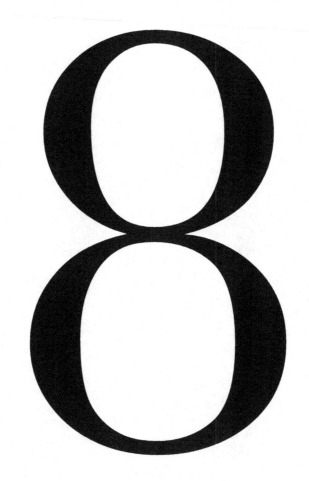

THIS IS THE NUMBER **EIGHT!**

EIGHT

THIS IS THE WORD **EIGHT!**

HERE ARE **EIGHT** CIRCLES!

THIS IS THE NUMBER **NINE!**

NINE

THIS IS THE WORD **NINE!**

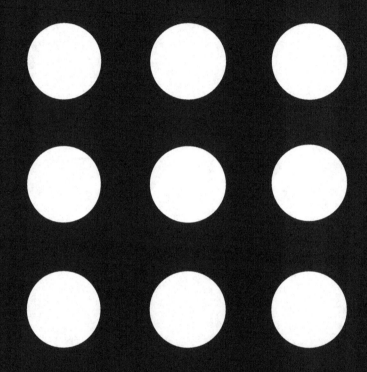

HERE ARE **NINE** CIRCLES!

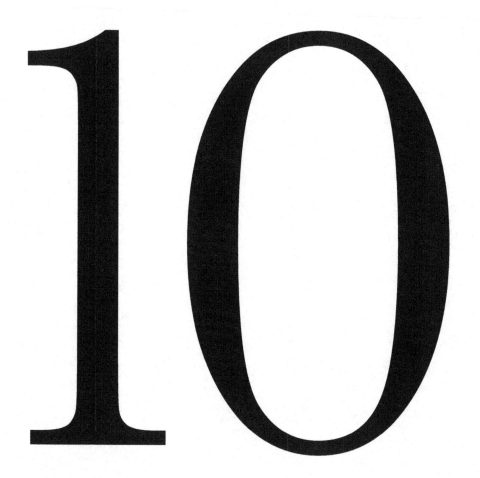

THIS IS THE NUMBER **TEN!**

TEN

THIS IS THE WORD TEN!

HERE ARE **TEN** CIRCLES!

THIS IS THE NUMBER **ELEVEN!**

ELEVEN

THIS IS THE WORD **ELEVEN!**

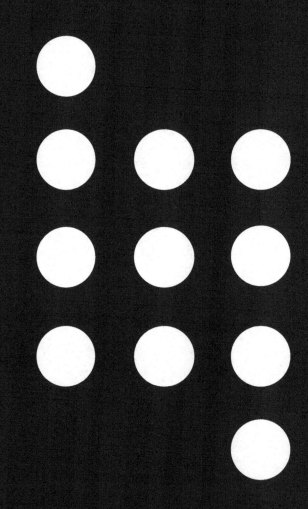

HERE ARE **ELEVEN** CIRCLES!

THIS IS THE NUMBER **TWELVE!**

TWELVE

THIS IS THE WORD **TWELVE!**

HERE ARE **TWELV**E CIRCLES!

THIS IS THE NUMBER **THIRTEEN!**

THIRTEEN

THIS IS THE WORD **THIRTEEN!**

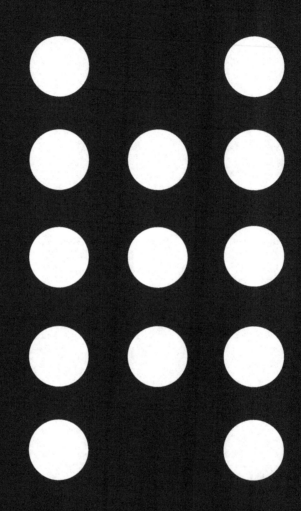

HERE ARE **THIRTEEN** CIRCLES!

THIS IS THE NUMBER **FOURTEEN!**

FOURTEEN

THIS IS THE WORD **FOURTEEN**!

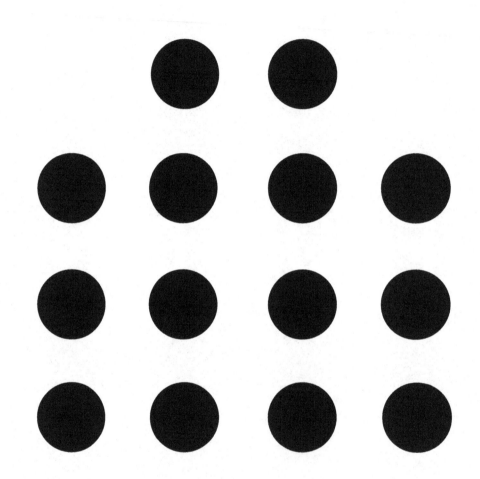

HERE ARE **FOURTEEN** CIRCLES!

THIS IS THE NUMBER **FIFTEEN!**

FIFTEEN

THIS IS THE WORD **FIFTEEN!**

HERE ARE **FIFTEEN** CIRCLES!

THIS IS THE NUMBER **SIXTEEN!**

SIXTEEN

THIS IS THE WORD **SIXTEEN**!

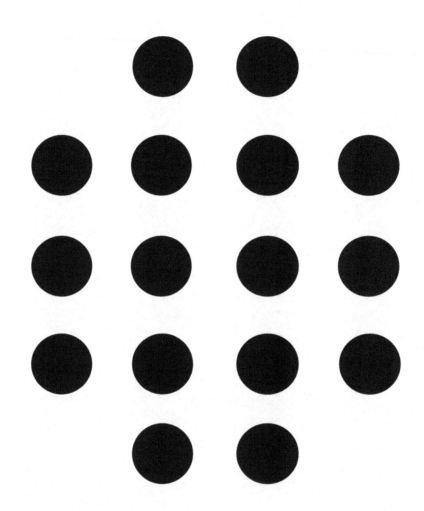

HERE ARE **SIXTEEN** CIRCLES!

THIS IS THE NUMBER **SEVENTEEN!**

SEVENTEEN

THIS IS THE WORD **SEVENTEEN!**

HERE ARE **SEVENTEEN** CIRCLES!

THIS IS THE NUMBER **EIGHTEEN!**

EIGHTEEN

THIS IS THE WORD **EIGHTEEN!**

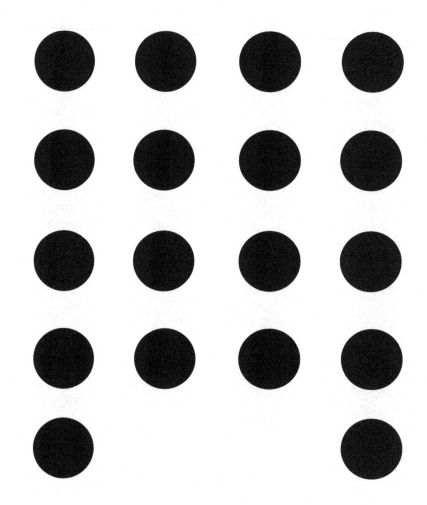

HERE ARE **EIGHTEEN** CIRCLES!

THIS IS THE NUMBER **NINETEEN!**

NINETEEN

THIS IS THE WORD **NINETEEN!**

HERE ARE **NINETEEN** CIRCLES!

THIS IS THE NUMBER **TWENTY!**

TWENTY

THIS IS THE WORD **TWENTY!**

HERE ARE **TWENTY** CIRCLES!

THIS IS THE NUMBER **TWENTY-ONE!**

TWENTY-ONE

THIS IS THE WORD **TWENTY-ONE!**

HERE ARE **TWENTY -ONE** CIRCLES!

THIS IS THE NUMBER **TWENTY-TWO!**

TWENTY-TWO

THIS IS THE WORD **TWENTY-TWO**!

HERE ARE **TWENTY-TWO** CIRCLES!

THIS IS THE NUMBER **TWENTY-TREE!**

TWENTY-THREE

THIS IS THE WORD **TWENTY-THREE!**

HERE ARE **TWENTY-THREE** CIRCLES!

THIS IS THE NUMBER **TWENTY-FOUR!**

TWENTY-FOUR

THIS IS THE WORD **TWENTY-FOUR!**

HERE ARE **TWENTY-FOUR** CIRCLES!

THIS IS THE NUMBER **TWENTY-FIVE!**

TWENTY-FIVE

THIS IS THE WORD **TWENTY-FIVE**!

HERE ARE **TWENTY-FIVE** CIRCLES!

THIS IS THE NUMBER **TWENTY-SIX!**

TWENTY-SIX

THIS IS THE WORD **TWENTY-SIX!**

HERE ARE **TWENTY-SIX** CIRCLES!

THIS IS THE NUMBER **TWENTY-SEVEN!**

TWENTY-SEVEN

THIS IS THE WORD **TWENTY-SEVEN!**

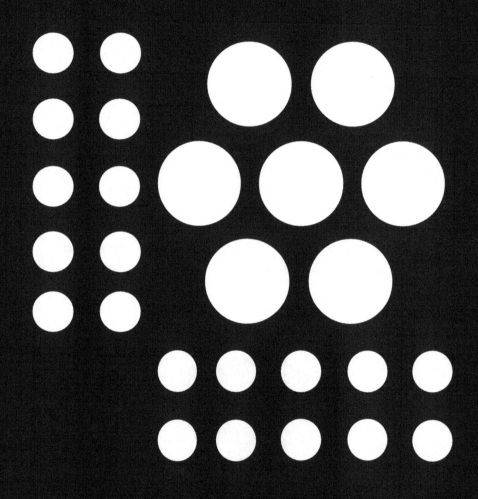

HERE ARE **TWENTY-SEVEN** CIRCLES!

THIS IS THE NUMBER **TWENTY-EIGHT!**

TWENTY-EIGHT

THIS IS THE WORD **TWENTY-EIGHT!**

HERE ARE **TWENTY-EIGHT** CIRCLES!

THIS IS THE NUMBER **TWENTY-NINE!**

TWENTY-NINE

THIS IS THE WORD **TWENTY-NINE!**

HERE ARE **TWENTY-NINE** CIRCLES!

THIS IS THE NUMBER **THIRTY!**

THIRTY

THIS IS THE WORD **THIRTY!**

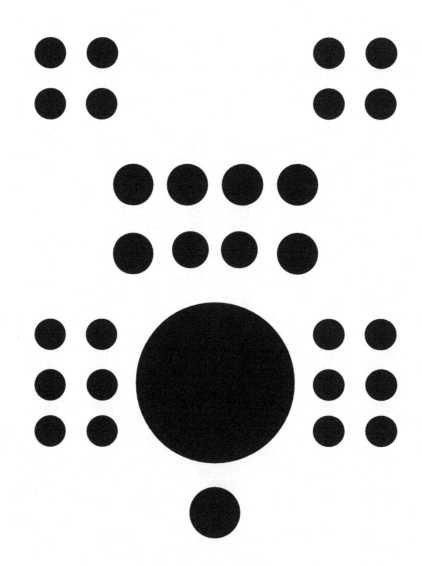

HERE ARE **THIRTY** CIRCLES!

THIS IS THE NUMBER **THIRTY-ONE!**

THIRTY-ONE

THIS IS THE WORD **THIRTY-ONE!**

HERE ARE **THIRTY-ONE** CIRCLES!

THIS IS THE NUMBER **THIRTY-TWO!**

THIRTY-TWO

THIS IS THE WORD **THIRTY-TWO**!

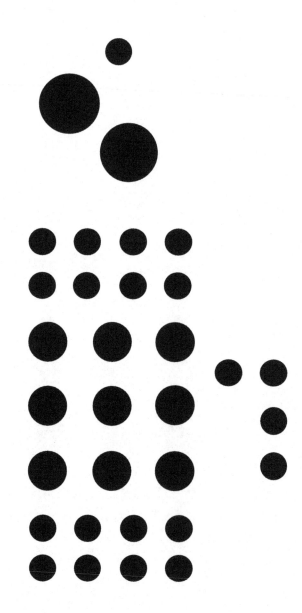

HERE ARE **THIRTY-TWO** CIRCLES!

THIS IS THE NUMBER **THIRTY-THREE!**

THIRTY-THREE

THIS IS THE WORD **THIRTY-THREE**!

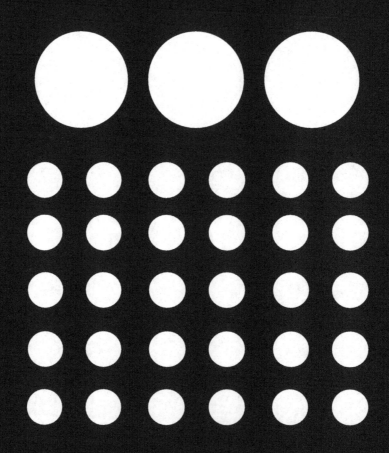

HERE ARE **THIRTY-THREE** CIRCLES!

34

THIS IS THE NUMBER **THIRTY-FOUR!**

THIRTY-FOUR

THIS IS THE WORD **THIRTY-FOUR!**

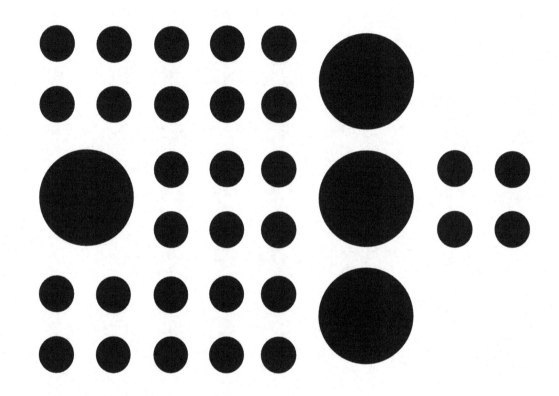

HERE ARE **THIRTY-FOUR** CIRCLES!

35

THIS IS THE NUMBER **THIRTY-FIVE!**

THIRTY-FIVE

THIS IS THE WORD **THIRTY-FIVE!**

HERE ARE **THIRTY-FIVE** CIRCLES!

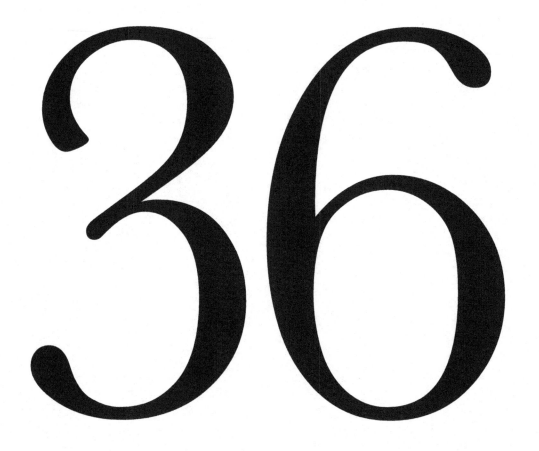

THIS IS THE NUMBER **THIRTY-SIX!**

THIRTY-SIX

THIS IS THE WORD **THIRTY-SIX!**

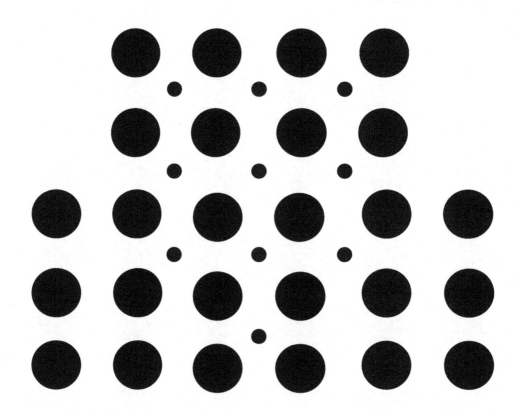

HERE ARE **THIRTY-SIX** CIRCLES!

THIS IS THE NUMBER **THIRTY-SEVEN!**

THIRTY-SEVEN

THIS IS THE WORD **THIRTY-SEVEN!**

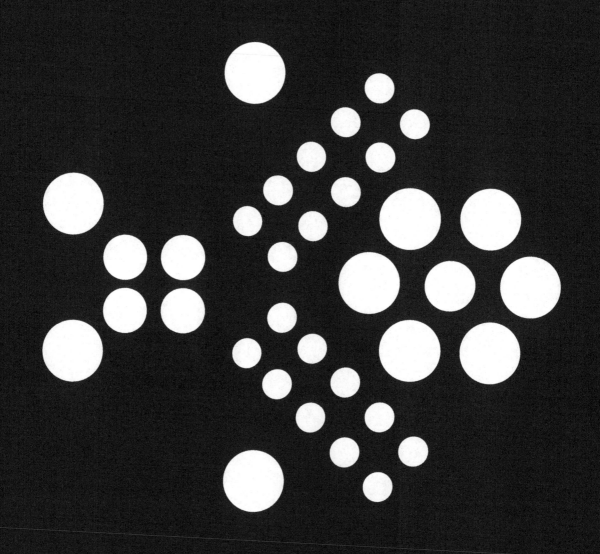

HERE ARE **THIRTY-SEVEN** CIRCLES!

THIS IS THE NUMBER **THIRTY-EIGHT!**

THIRTY-EIGHT

THIS IS THE WORD **THIRTY-EIGHT**!

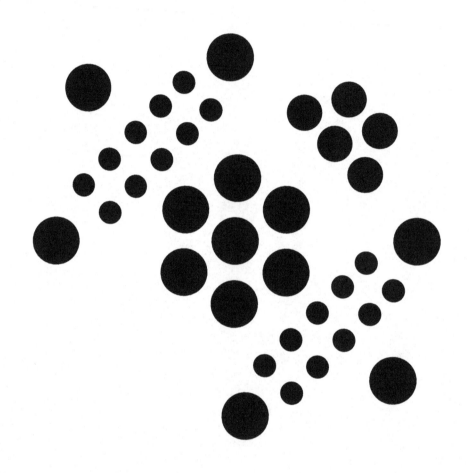

HERE ARE **THIRTY-EIGHT** CIRCLES!

THIS IS THE NUMBER **THIRTY-NINE!**

THIRTY-NINE

THIS IS THE WORD **THIRTY-NINE!**

HERE ARE **THIRTY-EIGHT** CIRCLES!

THIS IS THE NUMBER **FORTY!**

FORTY

THIS IS THE WORD **FORTY**!

HERE ARE **FORTY** CIRCLES!

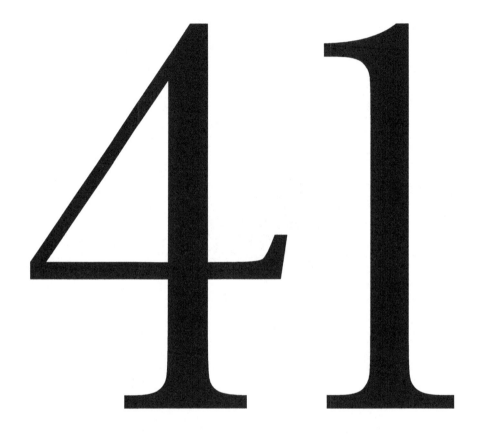

THIS IS THE NUMBER **FORTY-ONE!**

FORTY-ONE

THIS IS THE WORD **FORTY-ONE!**

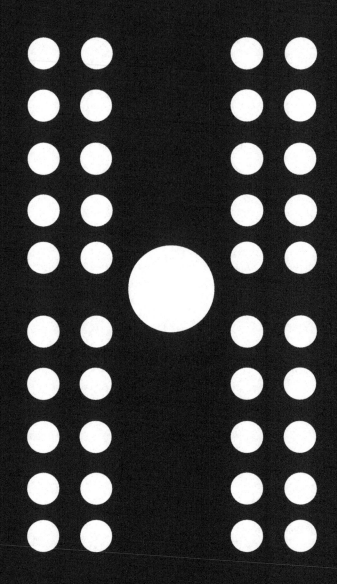

HERE ARE **FORTY-ONE** CIRCLES!

THIS IS THE NUMBER **FORTY-TWO!**

FORTY-TWO

THIS IS THE WORD **FORTY-TWO**!

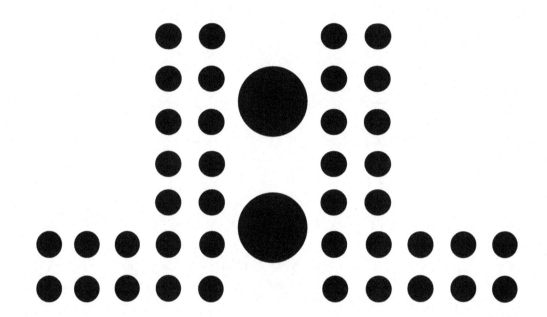

HERE ARE **FORTY-TWO** CIRCLES!

THIS IS THE NUMBER **FORTY-THREE!**

FORTY-THREE

THIS IS THE WORD **FORTY-THREE**!

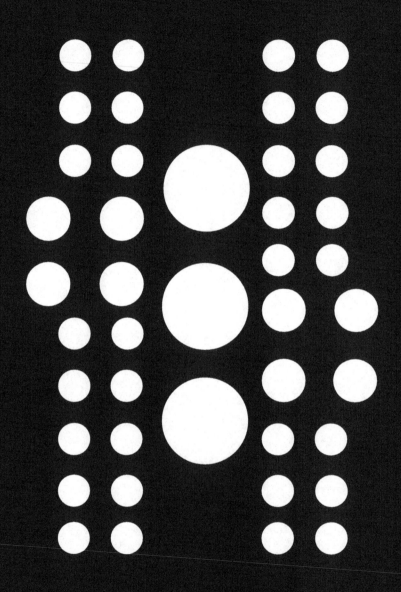

HERE ARE **FORTY-THREE** CIRCLES!

THIS IS THE NUMBER **FORTY-FOUR!**

FORTY-FOUR

THIS IS THE WORD **FORTY-FOUR**!

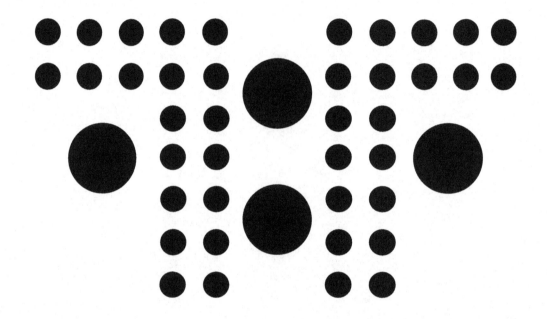

HERE ARE **FORTY-FOUR** CIRCLES!

THIS IS THE NUMBER **FORTY-FIVE!**

FORTY-FIVE

THIS IS THE WORD **FORTY-FIVE!**

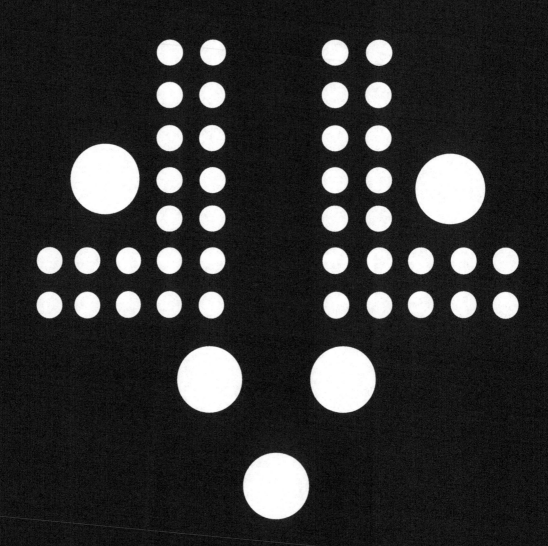

HERE ARE **FORTY-FIVE** CIRCLES!

46

THIS IS THE NUMBER **FORTY-SIX!**

FORTY-SIX

THIS IS THE WORD **FORTY-SIX**!

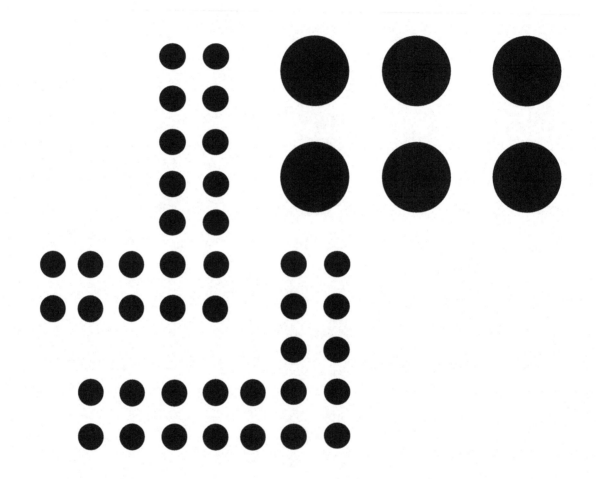

HERE ARE **FORTY-SIX** CIRCLES!

THIS IS THE NUMBER **FORTY-SEVEN!**

FORTY-SEVEN

THIS IS THE WORD **FORTY-SEVEN**!

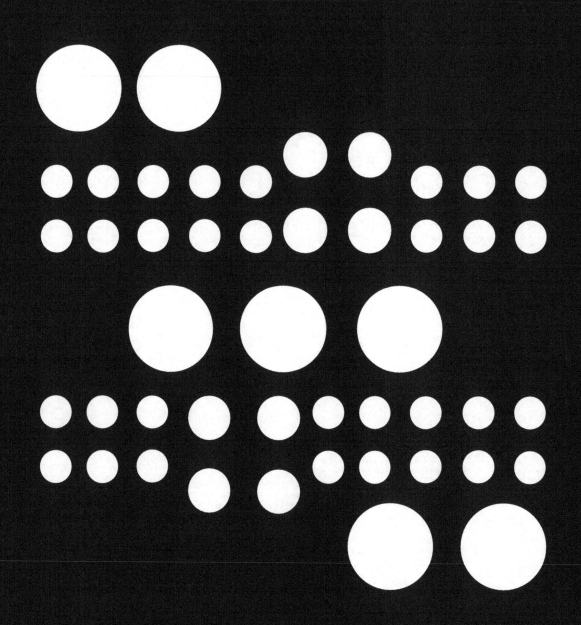

HERE ARE **FORTY-SEVEN** CIRCLES!

48

THIS IS THE NUMBER **FORTY-EIGHT!**

FORTY-EIGHT

THIS IS THE WORD **FORTY-EIGHT**!

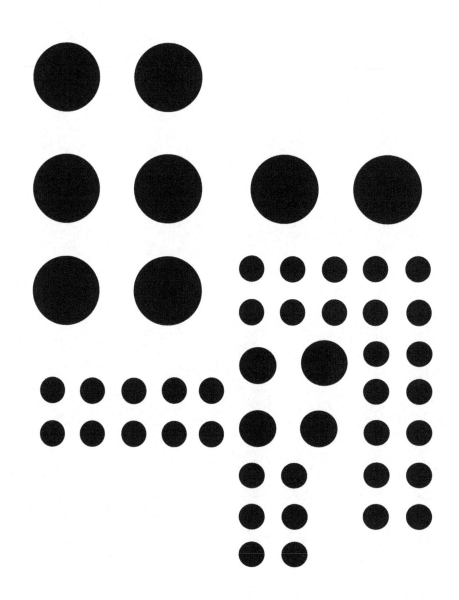

HERE ARE **FORTY-EIGHT** CIRCLES!

49

THIS IS THE NUMBER **FORTY-NINE!**

FORTY-NINE

THIS IS THE WORD **FORTY-NINE**!

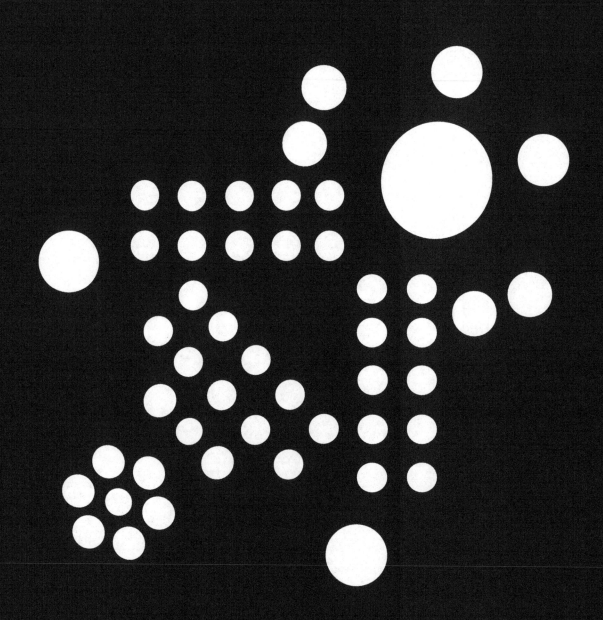

HERE ARE **THIRTY-NINE** CIRCLES!

50

THIS IS THE NUMBER **FIFTY!**

FIFTY

THIS IS THE WORD **FIFTY**!!!

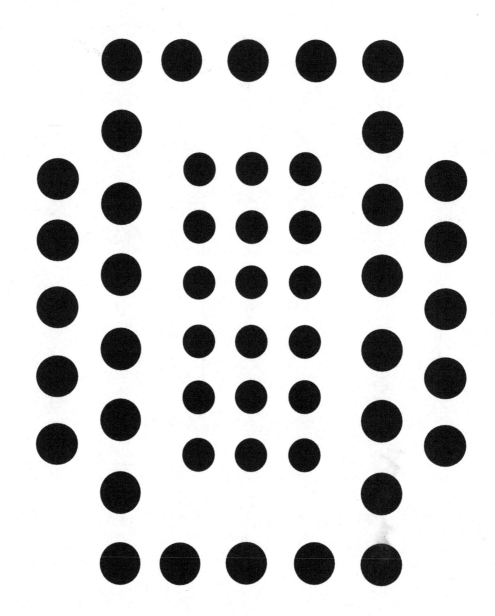

HERE ARE **FIFTY** CIRCLES!

YOU COUNTED TO
FIFTY!

GREATJOB!

Made in United States
Orlando, FL
29 November 2021

10899348R00115